W9-CMI-196

4-27-19

LONELY

by Kerry Dinmont

Published by The Child's World®
1980 Lookout Drive • Mankato, MN 56003-1705
800-599-READ • www.childsworld.com

Photographs ©: Shutterstock Images,
cover, 1, 4, 5, 6, 8, 16, 22 (bottom left);
Oksana Shufrych/Shutterstock Images, 9;
Wave Break Media/Shutterstock Images,
10, 18; Petrychenko Anton/Shutterstock
Images, 13; Dmytro Zinkevych/Shutterstock
Images, 14; Fat Camera/iStockphoto, 17;
Monkey Business Images/iStockphoto, 21;
iStockphoto, 22 (top left), 22 (bottom right);
J. Bryson/iStockphoto, 22 (top right)

Design Elements: Shutterstock Images

ISBN Hardcover: 9781503828117
ISBN Paperback: 9781622434718
LCCN: 2018944233

Printed in the United States of America
PA02395

ABOUT THE AUTHOR

*Kerry Dinmont is a children's book
author who enjoys art and nature.
She lives in Montana with her two
Norwegian elkhounds.*

CONTENTS

SAM IS LONELY

It is Sam's first day at school.

He doesn't know anyone yet.

He wants to make friends.

Sam's class goes outside at recess. No one asks Sam to play. He stands alone. Sam feels lonely.

BEING LONELY

People may feel lonely when they are alone. They also feel lonely when people **ignore** them. Everyone feels lonely sometimes.

You may feel an **ache** in your chest if you are lonely. You may feel **tired**. You might get sad. You might cry.

THINK ABOUT IT

What has made you feel lonely in the past?

It is okay to feel lonely. Some people might not know you are lonely. Ask a friend to come play. Reading a book might make you less lonely, too.

It is okay to be alone sometimes. At times you might want to be alone. You can have fun playing alone sometimes.

HELPING OTHERS

Other people get lonely. They might be sitting by themselves. They might look sad.

Go sit with them. Or ask them
to join you and your friends.

Making other people happy can make you happy, too.

WHO IS LONELY?

Can you tell who is lonely? Turn to page 24 for the answer.

A

B

C

D

GLOSSARY

ache (AKE) An ache is a mild yet ongoing pain. Being lonely might make you feel an ache in your chest.

ignore (ig-NOR) To ignore something means to not pay attention to it. When people ignore you, you might feel lonely.

tired (TIE-erd) Someone who is tired does not have much energy. Being lonely can make you feel tired.

TO LEARN MORE

Books

Dinmont, Kerry. ***Dan's First Day of School: A Book about Emotions***. Mankato, MN: The Child's World, 2018.

Kawa, Katie. ***I Feel Lonely***. New York, NY: Gareth Stevens Pub., 2013.

Shepherd, Jodie. ***How Do You Feel?*** New York, NY: Children's Press, 2015.

Web Sites

Visit our Web site for links about being lonely:
childsworld.com/links

Note to Parents, Teachers, and Librarians: We routinely verify our Web links to make sure they are safe and active sites. So encourage your readers to check them out!

INDEX